Fun with My Family

Annabelle Tan

Illustrated by Naomi Lewis

This is my grandfather.
We like to fish together.

This is my grandmother.
We like to ride bikes together.

This is my father.
We like to read together.

Mom's
Surprise

Daniel Lee
Illustrated by Naomi Lewis

This is my mother.
We like to dance together.

8

This is my brother.
We like to play together.

This is my family.
We like to have fun together!